Disappeared

Rita Richardson Jackson

Copyright © 2016 Rita Richardson Jackson

All rights reserved.

ISBN-10: 1530903491

ISBN-13: 978-1530903498

DEDICATION

This book is dedicated to women everywhere. Especially to women that have ever had a man to "ghost" out or disappeared on them

TABLE OF CONTENTS

1 Mistake #1 Misunderstood Atraction................1

2 Mistake #2: You're Being Too Proactive..............3

3 Mistake #3: You Worry Too Much About Getting Hurt Again..............5

4 Self Defined..............7

5 Solid Foundation..............10

6 Desirable Traits..............13

7 Hot Girl Energy..............17

8 Position Yourself..............20

9 Be Hard To Get And Get The Guy..............23

10 Awesome Self 24/7..............25

11 No Dating Before..............28

12 Sex: Never On Dates: Rules For Dates 1, 2 Or 3 And Why..............32

13 Never Put Yourself Into Volutary Relationship Lock-Down..............36

14 Relationship Markers..............39

15	Embrace High Value Traits (Of Women Of The Marrying Kind)	44
16	Never Give Away Your Most Precious Asset For Free!	47
17	Memo Of Understanding	50
18	The Rules: Act Like A Woman Don't Over-Extennd Yourself	52
19	First Date Perceptions	59
20	Is He Out Just For Sex?	62
21	Signs That A Man Is Ready And Interested In Developing A Relationsip With You	68
22	Keep His Interest Peaked	70
23	When Dating Rules Are Broken	71
24	Pressure To Have Sex	77
25	Is He Serious About You	78
26	Things That Will Make Him Want To Stay With You	80
27	Fantasy Versus Reality	82
28	First Impression Tips	85
29	Boyfriend Traits That Match Alpha Females:	89
Final Note		95
About The Author		98

ACKNOWLEDGMENTS

Thank you to my family and friends for continuing to accommodate my demanding schedule.

INTRODUCTION

Disappeared, is Rita Jackson's newest relationship book, and this book is available in hard copy and the eBook is quickly obtainable as an immediate download to your computer.

Even if you haven't dated around much, you've probably noticed patterns in your behavior that may have made you wonder about your dating and relationship choices! This may be the result of that the way your guy chooses to exit: It always seem to end in the guy you like, opting out (ghosting), or simply disappearing.

You tend to be attracted to handsome/cute, charismatic, alpha males. You have an aversion to nice guys and they tend to bore you. You desire to find a man who is taller, smarter, more generous, and more successful than you. You refuse to settle with the wrong guy, no matter what, right?

You feel like you've learned a lot, yet the results are always the same:

You don't want the men who do want you.

You want the men who don't want you.

And after the latest disappearing act from a man who really seemed like he cared, you've just about had it. You're determined to figure out WHY this keeps happening, WHAT you can do to prevent it, and HOW to avoid men who will (if given the opportunity) break your heart.

But, for the life of you, you can't figure this puzzle out.

You know you're a great catch.

You know that you've got a lot to offer.

You know that you're smart, interesting, independent, and passionate.

All you're looking for is a man who has all of these qualities as well. Is that so wrong?

Of course not! Really, you deserve it!

Still, Everywhere You've Turned For Advice, You Haven't Learned A Thing You Didn't Already Know!

Your friends, your family, women's magazines, dating books, talk shows, life coaches, and everyone reminds you that you're a goddess, a princess, a diva. Love will find you when you least expect it! Don't waste the pretty!

And yet here you are, at the end of your rope, after spending one month, three months, six months, one year, WASTING your precious time on another man who disappeared. STOP!

Your questions have been heard and answered, finally, in "Before He Disappears," by Rita Richardson Jackson.

Before He Disappears is the ultimate "Commitment Blueprint" facilitator because it is based on real conversations with men that have stayed in dating and relationships with women that I have consulted with me online, or in phone sessions. Before He Disappears is about what makes men fall madly in love with some women and completely vanish on others.

Before He Disappears is a great self-help resource, because it reads like a conversation with a good friend, but Rita Jackson just so happens to be a certified professional dating coach with many of the answers you need to whip your love life into shape!

There are plenty of finger-wagging "gurus" out there who will dish out the tough love. But who wants lectures when you're confused and hurting? With a unique combination of charm, wit and wisdom, Rita Jackson delivers the message you need to hear to get the love you want.

My name is Rita Jackson and I'm a dating coach who has written two previous books on relationships, and coached thousands of women to better understand the men that they are attracted to for love. Before getting married myself, I was a deliberate dater. And I have been courted by more than a few alpha personality men, that would by most dating standards be an ideal "catch!"

In other words, I'm not just a professional dating coach, I'm also a woman that have had guys try to court/date me, after, they have disappeared from women just like many of you reading this information, right now. Yes, you know the type: He is the guy who seemed like he was really into you, but was having second thoughts in his head the whole time, and finally split- out on you.

And, to be clear, I'm speaking about – quality men – who have done the exact same thing as the players, stringers, (or jerks). They are smart, kind, successful, and many are as relationship-oriented as you and I are.

However, there are a few major mistakes that the most impressive women routinely make, which drive men to seek out other relationships.

After 25 years plus of coaching, I have narrowed it down to the three biggest ones, I've been able to identify, and I have put it in to a downloadable eBook: Before He Disappears. This is a short read, but very accurate!

The 3 Biggest Mistakes Women Make That Cause Men To Disappear is revealed in the chapters

that follows. However, at the end of the day, a big reason that men disappear is that women that they disappear from are valuing the wrong traits in them. If you feel your boyfriend has to be the perfect fit for you - and you try to mold him into one - he's going to disappear for a woman who loves him despite his "flaws." A man may forget what you say but he will always remember how you make him feel when he's with you. Therefore, choose conversations and activities that positively impacts his emotional needs and this will cause him to want to be around you more. Thus lessening the chances of having him to disappear, or ghost on you.

CHAPTER 1

MISTAKE #1: MISUNDERSTOOD ATRACTION

Believing That What Attracts Him to You is the Same Thing You Find Attractive in Him

You look great for your age. You're educated. You make your own money. You're smart, analytical, resilient, driven, ambitious, and independent. You know what you're worth and, after a few bad experiences, you've vowed never to compromise to be with anyone who isn't up to par.

Yet every once in a blue moon, you meet a man who makes the cut.

Your attraction is strong. Your connection is real. Your chemistry is white hot.

You dive into a relationship … and he breaks up with you a few months later.

Next thing you know, he's involved with another woman who isn't nearly as attractive, successful, or impressive as you are. And you scratch your head and wonder what head injury this man has suffered to choose such a woman.

Why would he give you up for her? It's completely confusing... unless you understand men. Then, it makes perfect sense!

Ladies, please, understand this:

What you're looking for in a man is NOT what he's looking for in a woman.

•He doesn't care if you're smarter than he is.

•He doesn't care what you do for a living or if you have a healthy bank account.

•He doesn't care if you're cultured and well-traveled and sophisticated about the finer things.

Thus, your strongest traits – your intelligence, your success, your independence, your drive – don't matter as much to him. He wants what he can't get from his male friends.

THIS IS WHAT A MAN WANTS

A man wants a woman who makes him feel good, who makes him feel loved and secure. He wants someone who makes him feel sexy and trusted.

Regardless of what you do for a living, how successful you are, or even how beautiful you are, if you don't consistently make him feel good when he's with you, he's going to disappear and find a woman who does.

CHAPTER 2

MISTAKE #2: YOU'RE BEING TOO PROACTIVE

When highly success women start to "over-function, she is NOT letting the man be the man! Men win you over by giving to you. Men ask you out. Men call you. Men pay for dates. Men initiate sex. Men ask for commitment. Men propose marriage. Men give. Women receive. Many times, strong women, extraordinary women, alpha-personality women do this:

Reverse this order by asking him out, initiating sex, asking for commitment, or proposing marriage, and a masculine guy will feel, well, emasculated.

Thus, if you want a masculine guy, your greatest move is to embrace your passive feminine side.

You may hate the word passive. You may think it sounds like a 1930's housewife, or a helpless little woman who can't do anything for herself. Not quite.

Being passive doesn't mean that you can't do anything proactive. It means that you're choosing not to do anything proactive, because being proactive during courtship is ineffective in making a man feel attracted to you. Here are a

few common examples of being proactive:

•You have a great date, you email him the next day to say you had a lot of fun.

•You haven't heard from him all weekend, you text him to make sure he's doing okay.

•You want to see him next week, you tell him his favorite band is playing downtown and you can get tickets.

•You're confused about where your relationship stands, you ask him where things are headed.

You think you're being real; he thinks you're acting clingy. Understand, the man of your dreams doesn't NEED to be pushed to be your boyfriend.

This is where disconnect is: You want men to actively pursue you. **But most men do not want to be actively pursued.** The only guys who do are really shy, really insecure, or really clueless about women. Most men will value you more if they have to win you over. That's what guys mean about a "challenge."

So step away from "The Rules," which tell you to refuse to return his calls or act like you're busy when you're not, and is embrace your receptive feminine energy. Do Not: Continue to push men for dates, commitment or clarity! If you do, you will continue to watch them run away.

CHAPTER 3

MISTAKE #3: YOU WORRY TOO MUCH ABOUT GETTING HURT AGAIN

You've probably been hurt by guys in the past.

One boyfriend may have cheated on you. Another may have dated you for three years but didn't want to get married.

Another might have been a friends-with-benefits guy who never wanted a relationship with you.

And because you've had these life experiences, you're determined to learn from them. You tell yourself that you're never going to find yourself in that position again.

So you become vigilant. You look for the signs. You seek "red flags" and instantly dismiss a man you even SUSPECT is going to be a player, a commitment phoebe or a wishy-washy loser.

You ask him probing questions on the first date, looking for chinks in his armor.

You make it perfectly clear about what you will or won't tolerate up front.

You ask where your relationship is going after the third date.

Then you wonder why he disappeared.

Here's the deal:

There are many men around you that are not heartbreakers looking for their next victim. It is never their goal to hurt you at any point in time. Like you, they're not sure what will make them happy. All of them have repeated (to me) that they will know it when they see it.

Therefore, it is better to give him the chance to reveal himself over time.

When you push your boyfriend (too hard) to know where things are going, too soon, and you'll quickly find that they're not going anywhere at all. Allow him the opportunity, and he will ask you, and do the pursuing.

CHAPTER 4

SELF DEFINED

This chapter is about you defining yourself before your guy or someone else does it for you!

TIPS ON EMBRACING YOUR FEMININTY (and other things that men love)

Nails

Get your nails done on a regular basis. Stick to a decent length, no 4-inch nails please. Look at other women of your same complexion. That will help you pick colors that look good on your shade of skin.

Toes.

Do your toes to match. You don't necessarily have to go all out and get a pedicure, but at least get your toes painted the same color as your nails. When they start to chip, take the polish off! Men love French

manicured toes and nails. (That seems to be a big favorite from the men interviewed.)

Shoes.

Most men love a woman in heels. Designer heels will get you far with a man. Steve Madden has some of the best shoes at a decent price. You have to be careful with shoes, if it looks too unique or too outrageous, men will probably think it looks corny (that goes for everything, not just shoes). The men also said if you wear knee length boots or higher, just know you look like a whore; but a sexy whore and men love it!!!

Walk.

When you enter a room, take your time. Practice your walk and confident gaze across the room. Move your hips a little, too. Just assume that men will be watching and observing your curves, hips, thighs and butt stylishly cross their line of sight when you walk by.

Hair

Ladies: short hair accentuates every minute detail of the face Therefore, it is up to your judgement to choose a length and style better for you. However, many of the guys that I've spoken with favors medium (shoulder-length) to short hair, and tend to be easily attracted to women with long hair.Make Up. The less makeup the better.

Fake Lashes.

If you're brave enough and you really want to be a vixen, wear fake lashes. They can really make a world of difference, especially for special events. Don't buy them at the dollar store! You'll look really stupid if your eye lash starts falling off! Get them done at a licensed salon to avoid embarrassing mishaps.Stick to the short or medium lengths, as the long ones may be too much eyelash for most. Work

Out. Ugh, the dreaded dieting and exercise! It doesn't hurt to work out and eat healthy. There, I said it. If you need to shape up, just do it! I'm doing it, too. We can do it together. HOWEVER, don't let being overweight or having an out of shape body discourage you from practicing the techniques in this book.

This book will work for you regardless if you are skinny, fat, or in between. Look your best. Dieting and exercising is especially important if you feel bad about yourself. If you embrace your figure, and have confidence regardless of your weight, you're good. The only time being overweight will be a problem, is if it makes you unable to carry yourself with confidence. You've seen big women with their boyfriends, right, and thought to yourself, what the hell? Well, it's because they have confidence. Their weight doesn't stop them from being sexy and confident. If you can carry yourself like that, then weight isn't an issue for you. But, if you can't then you HAVE to get yourself to a place where you're able to have that confidence, because it is absolutely necessary

Breasts.

All of the men interviewed agreed on one thing: they love breasts. They are valuable treasures to a man, so don't be afraid to highlight them.

Hygiene.

Clean and freshen yourself, daily, and remove hair all excessive body hair

CHAPTER 5

SOLID FOUNDATION

Do you know what you want?

Never start new relationships while you are still angry or hurt about previous ones, but won't admit it.

If you ignore this rule, you set yourself up to expect a new or potential partner to ***prove you wrong*** about all your negative ideas about love.

Take yourself out of "relationship auto-pilot!"

This is the type of relationships where women (and some men) do what they do because they've been doing it, not because it gets them the happiness their hearts actually long for.

Having a "break-up – break-down, is another group of individuals that are putting themselves to sleep night after night with tears in their ears, surrounded by darkness, silently suffering while lying next to someone they've been having sex with for years and yet they **still** feel totally disconnected.

Another small group of individuals who get into relationships wanting emotional availability that they are not willing to reciprocate.

They claim they don't know how to love because their sorry family and/or relationship history never taught them how to **be in love**, but that doesn't stop them from eliciting emotional attachment from you because **they want the commitment experience without the commitment responsibility.**

Here are some of the most common ways relationships crash and fail, so beware:

Fear –

Going into a relationship with the primary goal of protecting your heart above all else; perpetually waiting for the other shoe to drop; looking for something to go wrong; creating something wrong if it doesn't happen soon enough on its own.

Toxic self-esteem –

Toxic self-esteem happens when someone with a low opinion of themselves in some way creates ways to force anyone who even *wants* to love them to have the same low opinion.

Dishonesty –

First with self, then by extension, about self to others. This makes intimacy a total impossibility no matter the **performance** of the partner. No matter how many hoops are successfully cleared, it will never be **enough** because you're in love with someone who doesn't exist; with someone your mate created in order to get you to **fall in love** with them, even though they very likely have no real intention of loving you back.

Here's the good news: Even if you've been doing these things for a lifetime, there's still a way out.

Your past does **not** have to be your future. Connect with me, 24/7, with your questions. Visit my website and contact me, as an option, at www.livepersonexperts.com. Or you can continue to do what you have always done, and keep getting the same results! So how's that working out for you?

CHAPTER 6

DESIRABLE TRAITS

Most guys have learned to adjust the image they have in their mind of the ideal woman. No girl is perfect, and while deal breakers will always vary from guy to guy, there are some things that pretty much *every* guy wants.

1. Be Hard To Get, But Not Bitch.

She knows what it's like to make a guy work for it, but she's not cruel and will give him a chance if he's truly interested. She respects herself enough to not rush into anything without knowing he's for real, but once a guy proves himself, she's completely open to the possibility of love.

2. Not Afraid To Call Guys Out On Their Donkey-Doo.

While she can be open-hearted and kind, she's not afraid to shut down any guy who disrespects her, whether by lying, cheating, or just acting like an asshole. She stands up for herself and the people she cares about, and no guy has the power to make her complacent.

3. She Cares About Herself.

Her emotional, mental and physical well-being are of utmost importance to her. Healthy people come in all shapes and sizes, and she doesn't have to have the body of Jennifer Aniston to be considered in shape. Guys want to be with a girl who cares about her health, and that will come across more in what she does to stay active rather than the number on the scale.

4. She Takes Pride In Her Physical Appearance.

Guys have no idea how much work actually goes into the "natural" look, but they'd much rather a girl spent time on makeup that doesn't make her look like a completely different person. He still wants to recognize the person he wakes up next to.

5. She's Open and Affectionate.

The perfect girlfriend would never try to hide him away, or be ashamed to be seen with him. She's supportive, never naggy, and might even brag to her friends about how great he is once in a while. When they're together, she lets him know she cares and doesn't deal in emotional manipulation.

6. She Enjoys Sex and Trying New Things In Bed.

We all settle for sex that is less that satisfying sometimes. But if a guy is going to commit for the long haul with one girl, she sure as hell better be the best sex he's ever had (and vice versa, as well).

7. Not Hung Up On Her Own Insecurities.

Guys want to be with a girl who knows who she is and is happy with it. He doesn't want to have to turn the lights off during sex because she's worried about her flabby thighs. He doesn't want to have to always stand on the left in photos because she thinks one side of her face looks better than the other. Sure, there will be things she isn't 100% happy with, but she's able to see the bigger picture.

8. She Enjoys Looking Her Best – But It's Not All For Him.

Her outfit choices probably don't always revolve around a plunging neckline, but sometimes she'll choose something specifically because she knows he'll love it. To him, that means his opinion matters to her, and obviously she wants to turn him on. However, at the end of the day, she dresses up because it makes *her* feel sexy, and that's what's most important.

9. She Has Her Own Life.

No guy wants to start dating a girl and have her suddenly claim all his friends as her own, move into his apartment, and start calling his mother "Mom." If he goes away for the weekend, she won't be texting him every five minutes, because she has plans of her own. She had a life before him, and she isn't going to toss it aside just because she's in a relationship now.

10. She's Not Afraid To Stuff Her Face In Front Of Him.

It may not happen frequently, but she's been known to eat him under the table once or twice, and she's fine with that. She'd rather indulge once in awhile and actually enjoy her food than obsessively count every calorie.

11. She's Unapologetically Real.

Guys want a girl who can be herself without worrying what other people think. She's may not be perfect, but doesn't need to be. She owns her flaws, and would never let a guy, or anyone else for that matter, make her feel like she's not good enough.

12. She's Drama-Free.

Most guys don't enjoy constant fighting. Girls who are drama magnets will reveal themselves early on, and they'll find themselves single soon after.

CHAPTER 7

HOT GIRL ENERGY

Just in case you don't have a clue, here are a few tips for you on how to "Up your game with Hot Girl Energy!" Of course how you look is important! However, don't focus entirely on your appearance! You have got to put in major effort and focus on your attitude. Cultivate self-confidence by acting like a woman with options. The more you behave like a desirable, sought-after woman, the more men will perceive you as being just that.

Here are a few "**Rules Girl**" thoughts about the differences between hot girls and those that are forgettable, aka "not" girls. Which one are you: Hot or Not?

1. A "not" girl plays hard to get. A hot girl is hard to get.

2. A "not" girl tries to prove her worth to a man. A hot girl expects a man to prove he's worthy of her.

3. A "not" girl slouches. A hot girl stands tall.

4. A "not" girl expects a man to complete her. A hot girl completes herself.

5. A "not" girl will try to change a guy. A hot girl won't date a guy

who needs to change.

6. A "not" girl nags when she doesn't get what she needs. A hot girl moves on.

7. A "not" girl makes a man the center of her universe. A hot girl has a life.

8. A "not" girl does the chasing. A hot girl gets chased.

9. A "not" girl tolerates being treated like an afterthought. A hot girl expects to be treated like a priority.

10. A "not" girl questions her own desirability when a guy isn't good to her. A hot girl doubts the guy's desirability.

11. A "not" girl will agonize over a guy's confusing behavior. A hot girl has better things to do.

12. A "not" girl avoids eye contact. A hot girl locks eyes.

13. A "not" girl sees herself through a man's eyes. A hot girl sees herself through her own eyes.

14. A "not" girl expects little and gets little. A hot girl expects a lot and gets a lot.

15. A "not" girl obsesses over her weaknesses. A hot girl defines herself by her strengths.

16. A "not" girl needs to be with a man. A hot girl chooses to be with a man.

17. A "not" girl revolves her life around a guy, making him want to run. A hot girl maintains independence, making him want to pursue.

18. A "not" girl ignores red flags. A hot girl runs.

19. A "not" girl values attention. A hot girl values respect.

20. A "not" girl works hard to keep a guy interested. A hot girl expects a guy to work hard at keeping her interested.

21. A "not" girl is an expert denial. A hot girl trusts her gut.

22. A "not" girl thinks her appearance is the key to keeping a man. A hot girl knows that being intelligent, interesting, and independent matter above all else.

23. A "not" girl will wonder whether a guy is into her. A hot girl thinks about whether she's into the guy.

24. A "not" girl focuses on what a guy says. A hot girl focuses on how he behaves.

25. A "hot" girl would rather be single than settle. A not girl is afraid to be alone.

26. A "not" girl obsesses on how she looks. A hot girl focuses on what she exudes.

CHAPTER 8

POSITION YOURSELF

Being single can sometimes cause anxious feelings in some women. And after a while, it can be tough to fight off visions of yourself choking to death on a grape in your tiny apartment, alone, surrounded by cats. Not only are these thoughts non-beneficial, but acting out in ways that show desperation, around men will cause them to disappear or ghost on you.

Admittedly so, and whether married or single, there are times when we're all guilty of entertaining thoughts like the ones that follow:

1. Everyone Else Is Coupling Up — I Must Be Doing Something Wrong.

You're not on a television reality show! — Falling in love is not a competition that involves waiting to be picked. And if it's not a competition, you don't need to worry about what everyone else is doing, right? Just because your girlfriends have found boyfriends or gotten engaged doesn't make them better than you. It just means their time came. Yours will come too and when it happens, it'll be *amaaaazing*... Focus on that. In the meantime, do ***you***.

2. I'm too picky — I should just settle.

As long as you don't have outlandish expectations — like, he needs to look like a model and be kind and be rich — you're probably not being too picky. You're probably just looking for a guy that fits well with you and that's okay. In fact, that's *exactly* what you should be looking for. Just because it's taking a while — which is no surprise because a real connection can take some time to find — doesn't mean you're doing something wrong. And the next time you catch yourself wondering if you want too much, remember: the biggest difference between people who have more and those who have less is that the ones who have more believe they deserve it. In other words, what **you** expect is a self-fulfilling prophecy. Accept less, become less, get less… Expect more, become more, get more. So, keep an open mind but **do not** settle for anyone that's not worthy of you.

3. I'm running out of time if I want to have kids.

We totally get it. The biological clock is a total bitch. But even if you don't find your boo by [insert your panic age here], that doesn't mean you're destined to be man-less and childless. Chances are you'll fall in love with plenty of time to spare — how many women do you know that never found anyone in spite of trying? probably not a lot — but even if you end up being a late bloomer in love, you'll be just fine because, these days, there are tons of ways to start a family once you're ready. Not only do plenty of women get pregnant naturally in their 40s and have healthy babies, but the ones that don't often find success with frozen eggs, IVF, donor eggs, surrogacy or adoption. So, instead of living in a panic, acting like you're going to turn into a pumpkin at midnight, relax… Being young and single is awesome — don't squander it worrying about something that will likely never even be an issue in the end.

4. If I Were Hotter / Skinnier /Smarter /More Interesting, I'd Have Someone By Now.

Insecurity is one of the most useless emotions. Think about it: What has it done for you lately? Not a goddamn thing, right? Except maybe bum you out and keep you down. And the worst part: because confidence is the single most attractive quality a person can have, focusing on your weaknesses actually makes you less attractive. No matter what you look like or what your shortcomings are, love yourself — the more you behave like a desirable woman, the more men will respond to you like one. So the next time you catch yourself having self-negating thoughts, tell yourself to STFU.

5. All Good Men Are Taken

No, they're not. Sure, it feels that way when you're going on crappy date after crappy date but remember: it only takes one. And like the princess in the fairytale, you're going to end up kissing a hell of a lot of frogs before you find him. That's not a bad thing — it's just the way it works. The frogs are lessons; they teach you what you want/need and help you become ready when the right guy appears. So don't get cynical. Rest assured that there's a fantastic guy out there who's trudging through his share of lame girls looking for YOU.

CHAPTER 9

BE HARD TO GET AND GET THE GUY

Playing hard to get is supposed to be the surefire way to land your crush. Of course, that's bullshit, because if you act like you have no interest in a man, he's going to find someone who does. That's why you have to alter your approach. You can still play hard to get, but you also need to be flirty and actually follow through in the end if you actually want to get the guy.

1. Tell Him You're Busy, But Suggest A Rain Check.

If you turn him down once, it could crush his ego. That's why you have to give him a little hope, even when you want to seem hard to get. That way, he won't give up on you and move on to the next girl.

2. Lean In Close, But Don't Touch Him.

If you want to tease him, lean in so close that your lips are almost touching, but don't kiss him. The mixture of anticipation and sexual frustration will drive him crazy. He'll be dying to put his hands on you.

3. Don't answer texts ASAP, but do answer.

If you refuse to answer his messages, why would he continue chasing you? Ignoring him will trick him into thinking you want him to leave you alone. That's why you should wait a while to text him back—just don't forget to actually do it.

4. Don't tell him your life story, but tell him a little.

You can try to act mysterious by revealing a tiny bit about yourself at a time. However, you shouldn't keep quiet when he's trying to have a conversation with you. If he asks you a question, answer him. Don't be rude.

5. Don't tell him how you feel, but do hint at it.

If you're trying to play hard to get, you don't want to tell your crush how badly you want to marry him — at least not right away. However, you should show a little interest. Give him flirty smiles and engage in playful banter. It'll encourage him to chase after you.

6. Tell him something about your weekend, but not everything.

If he asks you what you did last Friday night, you can make it sound more exciting than it actually was. That way, he'll think that you're a busy woman with tons of friends.

CHAPTER 10

AWESOME SELF 24/7

Men Decide pretty much everything about you in the first 30 seconds (and you can be awesome for 30 seconds, right, cupcake?

Men are made to love, protect, and be seduced by women. Just think about the emphasis on chastity belts and veils for women! These are ways to control a woman's "attractiveness" and desirability powers!

When you Meet a man and you like each other you will "synchronize" or click! There's chemistry there! This is a trait that scientist say happens innately.

The book "Marriage On Demand – Close the Deal: Marry Your Guy in 6 Months to a Year" explains how to capitalize on it so effectively, you and your guy will practically be dragged to the wedding alter!

The book is not a guide to finding eligible men, but explanations are given for how to behave once you've met them. The information is written so that you can bring him with you to the start line, and he will be able to walk a direct path to the wedding alter in 6 months to 1 year.

Even if you don't have a man, you can flip the odds of meeting a guy in your favor by going to places that singles (not married couples with kids) go: Join a gym, sign up with a dating service, Club Med or take a singles cruise vacation. You can also try churches, meeting a friend at a trendy restaurant where men hang out at the bar, go to book signings, college lectures, try taking up a male dominated sport like golf, tennis, putting a personal ad in a magazine or newspaper, and/or asking your friends for help.

SELF ASSESSMENT

Do a self-assessment of your physical appearance! What do you like about what you see?

What are your best features? Work it (your best features) to your advantage.

What to expect during transition

At times you may find it awkward to put the advice into action. Just realize that this uncomfortable feeling is part of changing.

Be brave enough to embrace the discomfort and move forward with practices and time, it will begin to feel normal. Just like learning to ride a bike, at first it seemed impossible! However, after a few practice runs you get the hang of it and now you can ride a bike with ease. Learning a new style of interacting with men and will be the same way!

Once you're able to let go of previous ways of thinking about men and dating, a completely new world awaits you. You'll have men lining up to date you, desperate for your attention, and eager to please you! You'll never be sad over men again you won't be cheated on lied to or let down by men ever again.

Your "Mr. Right" will find you! In fact, he may be someone that you already have a friendship with! Check out the men that already like you, and are always there for you! Trust me, you can easily make him fall madly in love with you, and never want to leave you. Best of all you'll be having the time of your life while doing it!

Since the beginning of time, men have had us (women) figured out. They know how to manipulate us, lie to us, cheat on us, play with our minds, and tear out our hearts! Even worse, is their ability to keep us around, even after they have done all of those terrible things! The question that begs an answer is: How did they get so good at it? And the answer is: They know our weakness, and that is -- our emotions.

CHAPTER 11

NO DATING BEFORE

COURTING

Courting is right on the "start-line" (at point zero) of the **Marriage On Demand Commitment Blue Print!** In fact, it is during the courting phase that a woman must control her emotions, and put into effect the **Marriage On Demand (MOD) Purposeful Dating Plan.** This is a no-nonsense approach to dating that helps a woman quickly weed out potential time wasters and stringers, before she gets too emotionally invested in them.

Dates, 1, 2, and 3 of the MOD-PDP, naturally, incorporates strategic questions that a woman can ask a new suitor, anytime that incudes but is not limited to meeting a man for the first time, or the man that you've been with for a while.

Pay attention to his answers to your questions, as well as his mannerisms (self-expression) too. Together, these two things will often reveal things about his integrity and honesty that may help a woman to decide if she leave him at relationship "start-line!" Not every man is marriage-minded or even ready to be in a relationship, and this is perfectly understandable. These are the guys that you must leave them where you found them, at "ground zero" on the relationship start-line, and keep it moving!

No matter how handsome (or hot) he is, you must control your emotions, and keep it moving! No matter how pretty he tells you that you are, sweetly acknowledge his feelings, but you must keep yourself positioned and free of time wasters and players, that are experienced at telling women just the right things (1, 2 3) to emotionally entrap them. You have the power within you to break the cycle of being the emotional victim, of yet another smooth talker.

Remember this: There are two (2) individuals in a relationship! YOU must take 50% of the responsibility (good or bad) of how your relationship turns out!

My best advice to you is to be patient and slow it way down. Take your time to make each date a purposeful one. Incorporate applicable relationship questions that will help you to answer these questions:

1. Is this man relationship minded, or is he just looking for a "THOT" (That Ho Over There)?
2. Right now, who / what am I to him?
3. What do I really know about him?
4. What do I want him to know about me?
5. Should I accept future dates with him?

Assume nothing. The courting phase continues until a woman has received a formal request to become a man's girlfriend, and she has said yes!

It is a time for newly introduced strangers to question each other and find out if they are compatible.

The courting phase is positioned at point zero (0)

On the MOD relationship continuum because this is an exploratory time, for both the man and woman. During this time of discovery, the woman must be patient and watchful of words and body language

Dates, one, two, three, four, and five is a perfect time for a woman to discuss her relationship boundaries, with her potential partner, and to engage in what I call "purposeful dating!"

When does the Courting Phase end?

The courting phase ends when the dating phase begins. The two phases are separated by the first relationship marker, that occurs when a man asks a woman to be his girlfriend.

In essence the courting phase ends when you accept a man's request to be his "official" girlfriend.

Becoming a man's girlfriend means that you and he may be viewed as a dating couple. During the courting phase, you are simply acquaintances getting to know each other.

It would be wise to engage in purposeful conversations, and strategic dates that will help a woman to decide if her suitor is a player, stringer, creeper, or keeper?

It is a time for a woman to control her emotions, stay alert for "red flags" that point to dishonesty or a lack of integrity. It is a time to weed out "Mr. Wrong," before getting emotionally or sexually involved.

Each relationship marker is an important part of the foundation on which the (MOD! Close the Deal: Marry Your Guy in 6 Months to 1 Year) **Commitment Blueprint is built.**

Plain and simply stated, it is the man's responsibility to do the asking, and not the woman.

Never again, will a woman have to wonder or ask this question: "Am I your girlfriend?" If you have to ask, then the answer is: no you're not!

And, as long as you are not his official girlfriend, you must not behave as if you are.

Behaving as if you are his girlfriend (or wife) when you are not, only puts a woman at an emotional disadvantage, and disrupts the natural steps of his commitment to you, and weakens the MOD Steps to the Wedding Altar Action Plan.

CHAPTER 12

SEX: NEVER ON DATES: RULES FOR DATES 1, 2, OR 3 AND WHY

What dates 1, 2, and 3 mean to a man: When a man asks you out for a second or third date, what it means is that he's interested in getting to know you better, because he felt a good connection with you on date #1. It doesn't mean that he necessarily wants to be "exclusive" or is thinking of committing to a "serious relationship," with you.

He's just enjoying your company, getting to know you, starting to wonder about you.

So what does that mean for you?

It means that the best thing for you is to do is the very same thing. Use those first few dates to simply get to know if you like this guy and if he's good for YOU.

Taking your time like this is good for several reasons:

- You get to make an informed decision about whether he's worth your time

- You prevent yourself from getting too wrapped up in a man before knowing if he IS worth it

- You protect yourself from getting your heart broken (if you're still checking him out and he breaks it off, you haven't yet determined if he was that great and worth the heart ache, right?)

So, even though guys do weird things, this is one instance where you should follow a guy's lead. Treat those early stages of dating just like a man: Take your time, have fun, and look out for you.

What If He Doesn't Call?

There are three reasons a man might choose not to pursue a relationship after those first few dates:

- He didn't feel the right connection with you

- He's emotionally immature and isn't ready for a relationship

He's a player and isn't capable of forming a relationship with you or anyone else.

One of the most important things for a woman to NOT do on the very first few dates, but especially the first date is to NOT have sex with a guy.

Sex

- Some women think they can hook a man with their great sex, foolishly believing he'll want to be with her because she's the nastiest and freakiest woman he ever met. Then there are the women that say they're just having sex "for fun" and they don't care about the guy, but then secretly get sad when he doesn't call anymore. Whatever type of girl you may be and whatever your reasoning is, having sex with a guy you like is the absolute WRONG thing to do. The trick is DO NOT HAVE SEX. The less a man gets, the more a man wants. Men only want you when they can't have you.

- You may think, "If two people like each other, then what's the problem?" Through a social media site, I asked men this specific question, "Why do guys convince women to give it up, but then treat her like a stranger when she does?" Well, in so many words it came out like this "Men don't treat a t.h.o.t. (That Ho Over There) like a lady of respect." Only a women that doesn't respect or value herself would have sex with man she barely knows on a first, second or third date.

Summary

- Set and Know your sexual boundaries! What would a man have to do to prove to you that he is your "ride or die" soul mate worthy of your body and a commitment to him?

COMMITMENT BLUEPRINT

Simply defined the Commitment Blueprint is a relationship resource / schematic diagram that may be referred to by singles interested in getting married. It does not guarantee that you will get engaged and married in 6 months to 1 year, but it will help you to pace your movement, on our relationship continuum, in deliberate steps guided by relationship markers. Until those markers have been reached, a couple must remain where they are without experiencing the benefits the next higher level on the relationship continuum.

This allows a man the opportunity to earn his woman's hand in engagement and marriage, as he and she demonstrates their mutual love, trust, loyalty and integrity (to each other).

CHAPTER 13

NEVER PUT YOURSELF INTO VOLUTARY RELATIONSHIP LOCK-DOWN

When you first meet a guy, he tells you many things that you want to hear, and your emotions are being satisfied on every level and from all directions. He's calling you, asking to take you out, and probably spending money on you, too. Just because he's doing these things with your and for you should not cause you to put yourself into "voluntary relationship lock-down!" In fact it would be a mistake to do so.

From the start, you must exercise patience, and allow him the time, and give him the space to show a willingness to **begin** a commitment to you.

The process of him (your guy) "locking you down, begins when he formally asks you to be his girlfriend. He is asking you to "go steady" with him.

Sometimes a guy will plan a romantic date, and give you a small diamond ring to celebrate this occasion.

Asking a woman to be his girlfriend is the first step in the "lock-down" process. It also initiate the male's journey of commitment (to you). He is asking you to accompany him out of the "courting" pool of suitors.

This is an important relationship marker, because it moves the two of you from the initial "courting phase" to the "Dating" phase.

However, officially dating each other as boyfriend and girlfriend does not guarantee exclusivity.

What it means to a woman can mean something totally different to a man. So, before a woman starts planning her wedding and looking up names for their first born, it's best to take a "chill pill" and relax.

Now is the time to engage **in purposeful dating** with your boyfriend, and to ask questions that can reveal his true intentions and his thoughts of where the relationship is going.

It is a period of discovery for both of you as a dating couple!

Each phone call, and date that you take should include meaningful questions that will help both of you to decide whether or not, spending more time together is what you want, or not.

It is perfectly appropriate for a woman to establish an "expiration" date for exclusivity, with him, especially if he says that he's not sure and / or he needs some time to "think about it."

A reasonable time to keep a woman on relationship lock-down, as her boyfriend, is 6 months, maximum. At the end of 6 months the boyfriend is expected to "bust a move in one direction or the other, and make his intentions known to her about his future with her.

If marriage to you is in his future, and he would like to keep you to himself, the next logical step for him to keep you on lock-down is to make it official, and "pop the question!"

If your boyfriend does not see marriage with you in his immediate future, and marriage is your goal, this is the appropriate time for you "fall back" and to re-enter the courting phase (with or with out him). You are well within your rights to interact with new suitors, while he figures out.

It is advisable to **not** engage in a sexual relationship with your boyfriend, during this exploratory dating phase, of 3 - 6 months, for reasons related to "emotional" investment, commitment, and the fact that he may turn out to be temporary (in your life). After your guy "pops the question," asks you to marry him, and puts an engagement ring on your finger, you may (with discretion) phase in some small levels of touching and kissing, etc. However, keep in mind that you are single until married. An engagement ring does not make you his wife. You are not obligated to perform wifely duties.

CHAPTER 14

RELATIONSHIP MARKERS

Relationship markers are action indicators that signals the appropriate movements along the continuum line, of a relationship.

Courting is the first **relationship marker** on the "start-line" of the relationship continuum. Dates 1, 2, 3, are in this category.
It is a time for newly introduced strangers to question each other and find out if they are compatible.

The courting phase is positioned at point zero (0) on the MOD relationship continuum because this is an exploratory time, for both the man and woman. During this time of discovery, the woman must be patient and watchful of words and body language

Dates, one, two, three, four, and five is a perfect time for a woman to discuss her relationship boundaries, with her potential partner, and to engage in what I call "purposeful dating!"

When does the Courting Phase end?

The courting phase ends when the dating phase begins. The two phases are separated by the first relationship marker, that occurs when a man asks a woman to be his girlfriend.

In essence the courting phase ends when you accept a man's request to be his "official" girlfriend. Becoming a man's girlfriend means that you and he may be viewed as a dating couple. During the courting phase, you are simply acquaintances getting to know each other. It would be wise to engage in purposeful conversations, and strategic dates that will help a woman to decide if her suitor is a player, stringer, creeper, or keeper?

It is a time for a woman to control her emotions, stay alert for "red flags" that point to dishonesty or a lack of integrity. It is a time to weed out "Mr. Wrong," before getting emotionally or sexually involved.

Each relationship marker is an important part of the foundation on which (the MOD! Close the Deal: Marry Your Guy in 6 Months to 1 Year Commitment Blueprint) is built.

Plain and simply stated, it is the man's responsibility to do the asking, and not the woman.

Never again, will a woman have to wonder or ask this question: "Am I your girlfriend?" If you have to ask, then the answer is no you're not! And, as long as you are not his official girlfriend, you must not behave as if you are.

Behaving as if you are his queen, when you are not, only puts you at an emotional disadvantage, and disrupts the steps to the wedding alter action plan.

A woman of the marrying kind, doesn't "play" hard to get, she is hard to get!

Men are hunters, and they fall in love with the challenge of working for (and earning) a woman's hand in marriage.

Each **relationship marker** has certain qualifiers that must be met, passed or demonstrated to advance and move forward to the next level of the relationship commitment blueprint.

Therefore, until a man asks a woman to be his girlfriend, and she has accepted his proposal to be his "girlfriend," then she is not. She is not to provide "girlfriend" benefits, or tell others that she is (his girlfriend).

A man that's into a woman will meet her standards and respect her boundaries, when she clearly makes them known, to him. The key, here, is that she has to make them known in her own charming way.

Becoming one man's "official" girlfriend is the relationship marker that initiates the dating phase, and a man's interest in becoming exclusive with her.

If you move along the MOD Commitment Blueprint you will naturally come to specific relationship markers that must be earned by "Mr. Right" along the way.

This is not a time for you to laugh off the Commitment Blueprint rules and allow your emotions to dictate the right time to have sex with your guy. Nor should you will let any man tell you when to have sex with him.

Listen, the kind of woman that a man will pop the question to, and marry, acts like a lady and controls her emotions, all the way to the wedding altar!

Keep in mind that you are free to continue courting other single available men, during the courting phase, too. Believe me, men do. In fact, some men will string several women along (at the same time) without any mention of what they are to him). In fact, each one of them thinks that she is his girlfriend! Often times, these women have given "girlfriend" and permanent, emotional benefits to men that should have been temporary men in their lives.

These are men that I refer to as time wasters and stringers that reap the benefits of being in a relationship without fully committing to being in one.

Your honesty with a man, and refusal to cross relationship boundaries, without specific markers in place, will make the right inference (to him) about your strength of conviction to stand on your values and high self-esteem.

Believe it or not, men are actually turned on by women that make them work to earn them, step by step, and often times triggers thoughts of him marrying this "high value woman," way before the woman knows it!

Men treat all women in the same way, and that is: the way women allows them too.

Every day, is a day to be awesome, and to represent your brand well! Your actions and the way that you carry yourself speaks volumes!

When marriage to your special guy is what your goal is, don't be so "thirsty" acting, and settle for gifts, trips and expensive vacations. Accepting these things rarely leads to anything other than premature intimacy, as a pay back!

Reminder: Control your emotions, and keep your emotional shield raised! Know the answer to this question: Who are you to him?
On the start line, you are his **Friend** (during the courting phase).
You will continue to be friends until he formally ask you to be his "girlfriend."

Be patient, and wait for him to ask you to be his girlfriend. He will, especially if you can control yourself and NOT assume the title, and start acting like one. And for goodness sake, do not have sex with him on the first, second, or third date! You are just new friends (and getting to know each other's boundaries). Engaging in any form of sexual activities is highly inappropriate for any woman. However, a true diva/queen with high esteem, high value, and self-respect would NEVER allow any form of intimacy during the courting phase, and especially having NOT been formally asked to be his girlfriend.

Reminder: Until the man asks you to be his girlfriend, you are NOT. Having sex with friendly random men during the courting phase is out of the question.

It doesn't matter how perfect a woman looks, she will be treated like a common t.h.o.t. (that ho over there) the minute she gives into a guy, without him putting in the EFFORT to prove that she is special to him.

Basically, men pretend they want a woman who "doesn't play games" and is "mature," and can handle sex with no strings, but these are just "player" lines to get a woman to go to bed with them, and to get you committed to them without them proving that they are committed to you.

CHAPTER 15

EMBRACE HIGH VALUE TRAITS (OF WOMEN OF THE MARRYING KIND)

- **Respect yourself.** To men, a respectful woman has boundaries. A woman with no boundaries, allows the man to set her boundaries according to his interests. He treats her in ways that demonstrates that she is there for his pleasure, and not for developing a loving relationship that leads to marriage. The tone in his voice when he speaks to you, the words that he speaks, the lack of use of cuss words in front of you, and his manners should always be on the respectful level with you in his presence.

- **Don't play "Hard to Get: Be hard to get!** Men want to get the girl that's a challenge and doesn't give it up easily. The girl that makes him wait for it, work for it, and chase after it. The (h.t.g.) **hard to get** woman is the woman they really want. This type of woman (the h.t.g. woman) is not playing hard to get games either! She **is** hard to get! A man knows and recognizes that a true queen or diva (of the marrying kind) is the woman that has no problem with rejecting a bull-shitter, in his tracts, including but not limited to him!

- **Show that you know that you don't have to have sex with a man for him to love you or marry you.** The woman he falls in love with is the exact opposite of a t.h.o.t., because men don't fall in love with a woman that is too easy! Men fall in love with ladies, queens and divas who are smart (relationship wise) enough to know they don't have to have sex.

- **Never act "thirsty"** or act like you want to have sex quickly, because it's an "unqueenly-like, un-lady-like, un-smart indicator that will weaken your brand, and render you "powerless!"

- **Make him put in some effort** to show that you are special and mean the world to him. The type of woman a man will love gives off a vibe that says loud and clear: "I'm not an easy t.h.o.t. - type of woman, and you're going to have to put in some effort, if you want a girl like me, because I'm very special."

- **Create an opportunity for him to demonstrate** his words of affection (that he has expressed to you). Test his loyalty to you, way before you give in to any one of his requests! Giving away your time, companionship, body, is never a wise thing to do, especially when your goal is for your guy to marry you! After all, "Why buy the cow when the milk is free," is an old theory that hints at this: if you get something free, you don't appreciate it as much as if you had to work for it. The harder he has to work to prove that he is committed to you, the sooner he will pop the question, and marry you!

- **Summary:** If a guy begs you and pressures you for sex from day 1, and you refuse to do it and he leaves you alone, he was just out to freak you and forget you, so aren't you glad you didn't give it up to him? I'm just keeping it real. If you deny a man sex and he doesn't continue to pursue you after you have rejected him; that is concrete proof he was never genuinely interested in YOU.

- ~ He was only looking for SEX. ~ Don't try to convince yourself it was anything less than him trying to use you. When you're out in the dating world, this is going to happen... a lot. So, don't take it personally when it happens. You have to take it for what it is: There are lots of players and stringers out there having a good time at the woman's expense. You can choose to fall into the category of "women who can be used," or the category of "women who cannot be used."

Fact: Marriage is not for everyone. And not every single woman wants to get married. However, if you are a single woman that is interested in getting married, YOU have to know (and stand confidently in) your worth. Before you find "the one," you may actually date several good potential partners, with whom you may have great chemistry. However, this doesn't mean that they deserve All you have to offer.

Word to the wise: It would be premature for YOU to give your All to each dating partner that you chose to be in a committed relationship with, before they have fully committed to you through engagement and marriage (if marriage is your goal). Of course if being a friend with benefits is about all that YOU think that you deserve, and you are willing to do everything that a wife does and more, you may find yourself single and eventually dumped, after years of being the perfect girlfriend/wifee.

CHAPTER 16

NEVER GIVE AWAY YOUR MOST PRECIOUS ASSET FOR FREE!

A woman's most precious asset is her body. No matter what, a woman must never give the key to her most precious asset to a man, especially one that may be temporary! The quickest way to have a guy "ghost" or disappear on you is to have sex with him, especially, on dates 1, 2,or 3. See the special chapter that discusses the rationale behind this hypothesis). To have sex or not (and when) is completely up to you. However, there are rules and consequences that may apply. Ideally, it is better to wait until you have evidence of commitment. Some women set up a rule of no kissing or hugging for the first dates. And there are other ladies that choose not to allow any fondling of an intimate nature until after a 90 day rule, and/or they are formally engaged! That's right! The man has to put an engagement ring on their finger, first!

- **Here's a tip for you:** If you're dating a man that takes your rejection (of no sex or intimate touching for the first 90 days) like a gentleman and is willing to wait, this is a sign he genuinely likes you for you.

- Keep in mind that, if you're just beginning to date and/or not fully committed, there's a chance your new guy may still may have someone on the side. **In all honesty, he's most likely going to get sex somewhere else if he's not getting it from you.** There are some things that you cannot control, and this is one of them! In his mind, she'll be "the easy t.h.o.t. that he is not going to marry, and you'll be the woman that gives him goosebumps when he sees you or thinks about you! And he will send you roses.

- **Don't be the woman that a man uses for sex,** while sending flowers and going out on nice dates with his "lady-friend."

- **When you choose to ignore certain relationship rules, and do what "feels" good, and seek to please a man:** You'll be the one hurt in the end, while she'll be "the one" who made him fall in love.

If you need support to follow the MOD Relationship Rules:

- Seek the help of a therapist or counselor, if you have issues with giving in to sex too easily or you're having a hard time "getting" this point: No sex with any guy until that guy has earned it through **a series of relationship markers that underscores a commitment to you.**

    ___ **He has passed your "Ride or Die" Test that he will assist you, protect you, respect your boundaries, and assist you in a time of need.**

- Do whatever is necessary to sink the following statements into your head permanently: Visualize that your vagina is something of value, and is therefore, under lock-down. **And for the sake of this example, only, not for real,** let's say that your vagina has a cash value of a crisp $1,000 bill. Would you give a man you just met a FREE $1,000 bill just because he ask for it sweetly? Of course, you wouldn't. If you need too, write it100 times until you memorize it, say no to sex for dates 1, 2, and 3, and it is best to put off any intimacy such as heavy kissing, too, for 60 - 90 days.

- Here's the rub: **A man that is Not that in to you" will not stick around.** Withholding sex until a later time will help you to protect your heart, and keep your body healthy and free of STDs, too.

Bonus: You will "weed out" the players, stringers, and time wasters at the same time!

- Giving up sex easily is the **exact wrong way** to use your power over men, because it renders you powerless, and will prevent you from knowing the guy's true intentions with you.

- Perhaps, you have been in a cycle of men having sex with you and "disappearing?" If so, **you will have to stop doing permanent things (like having sex with men that haven't proven themselves to you!**

- YOU must stop doing permanent things with individuals that turn out to be temporary: (players, stringers, and time wasters) You have to control your emotions, look for positive relationship markers, and keep your options open.

CHAPTER 17

MEMO OF UNDERSTANDING

- Until a man has passed certain relationship markers, **with you**, such as asking you to be his "official" public girlfriend, dated you for 90 days or longer without pressuring you to have sex, proved that he will be your "ride or die" when you need him, sex must remain off limits to him (**with you**)

- In reference to myself, and others that anonymously responded to my social media requests, for this book, males and females agree that men will marry the woman within 6 months to 1 year the woman is an advocate of marriage and family, and she includes that being in an "official" committed relationship as a "relationship marker, in the foundation of her Individualized Success plan.

- When a man loves a woman, he will do whatever it takes to keep her, including respecting her sexual boundary(ies). Ladies, make sure you have one in place. You must know what you will and will not do, in the name of love.

- If you are dead set on having sex with a man (before marriage) you must not allow any man access to your body until he has earned the right. I will say it again, because it is SO important:

THE CORRECT WAY TO USE THE POWER OF intimacy IS TO NOT GIVE IT UP FREELY. A MAN MUST EARN THE RIGHT TO HAVE SEX WITH YOU. HE MUST PUT FORTH EFFORT TO PROVE HE IS WORTHY OF YOU. Otherwise, You will kill your opportunity to become the woman he falls for and in love with, and/or you will prolong the time that it will take for him to put a ring on it, if at all. Therefore, if you really like him and hope to create a committed relationship with this particular man, then DO NOT HAVE SEX WITH HIM.

CHAPTER 18

THE RULES: ACT LIKE A WOMAN DON'T OVER-EXTENND YOURSELF

Have you ever found yourself falling for a man you were dating and wondered if he was feeling the same way? Did you find yourself trying to prove what a great catch you are by being sweeter, funnier and smarter in hopes that he would fall in love with you? Focusing on what a man wants and trying hard to be that woman may feel like the natural thing to do, but it's the worst way to try to make a man feel romantic love for you. Love isn't a reasonable emotion – and being "nice" and "understanding" and "a good sport" won't get you where you want to go. Here are some ways that will:

Rule # 1: Don't give a man more than he gives you

- Love, and inspiring a man to fall in love with you forever, is all about you being able to receive love.

- Most of us only know how to give. We give for lots of reasons – because we're taught that's the way to get to a man's heart (it isn't) because we see other women do it, and because deep down, it feels uncomfortable and scary to be vulnerable enough to really accept and to get love.

A man is actually turned off when he gets more from you than he gives. When you shower him with affection, attention, dinners, gifts, and always go out of your way to drive to his place, it makes him think of you as a mother or a friend instead of inspiring his emotional desire for you.

Rule # 2: Don't give away exclusivity if he hasn't yet committed: Exclusivity Does NOT Guarantee Commitment

We become totally, emotionally invested in a man when we're exclusive with him because he has all our time and attention. There's no way we can stop wondering about where the relationship is going. But the more we think about it and talk about it, the more we push a man away! Until he ask you to be his girlfriend, and you have answered yes, then you are just friends.

If you're dating or in a relationship with a man who hasn't yet fully committed to you, then you should keep dating other men.

Why? By doing so, you'll feel that you have choices and you won't invest all your time and energy into a man who isn't sure yet what kind of future he wants with you.

If he isn't sure, why are you? And marriage is your goal, stay focused! When he has told you HIS truth: He isn't sure, it is best to let him figure it out while you keep dating! Next!

Not surprisingly, this goes against everything women naturally believe about relationships.

Women have been taught since childhood to believe that becoming a man's "girlfriend" and being exclusive naturally leads to a long-term, committed relationship. This is a total lie!

Rule #3: Don't give him gifts, make him dinner or pay for dates

Yes, this sounds unfair, and yet, who pays is often the difference in his mind between friends hanging out together and a "date."

If a man complains about paying for everything, let him know that you don't really care about doing things that always cost him money. And that you feel great being with him, and you don't want to pay. Walking, hanging out in bookstores, having a picnic in a park can all be fun, romantic ways to get close to a man, anyway.

(And forget about cooking dinner, or trying to make dating "reciprocal." A bowl of popcorn and something to drink is fine.)

When you give a man gifts, give him all your attention and energy, and give MORE than you receive, you're OVERFUNCTIONING.

Over functioning is doing more than your fair share and stepping up to rescue a man because you know you can do a better job. It's arriving from your masculine energy. It feels aggressive and forward to a man. And it's totally unattractive to him. Over functioning triggers a negative

response in a man, and what to do to stop doing so much and instead get more love and more affection from your man by doing LESS.

Rule # 4 Make love to his mind, and the rest of him will follow!

Love bonding is vitally important between a man and a woman, when laying the foundation of the commitment blueprint.

Therefore, every date that you have with your guy will have a strategic purpose related to building that strong foundation on which your relationship is to be built.

The purpose of this game is to create and nudge along a lasting bond (of love) and is a part of the commitment blueprint.

Believe me, you will be happy with the results, since a man's mind is directly linked to his heart.

Rule # 5 Use each Date Strategically:

Go for a walk together, or do something to share with your partner.

When a woman practices proper dating and relationship etiquette a magical thing happens: Either a man will step up his game to fight off the competition, or he'll get lost in the shuffle. And this is how you make room for the real Mr. Right to show up!

Rule # 6 Don't do permanent things with temporary men.

Any man that straight out tells you that he's is not sure to commit to you, really isn't! This is NOT your "Mr. Right, right now! He is NOT the man to bring to the start line on your journey to the alter in 6 months to 1 year! No ma'am!

The truth is, the moment a woman makes a man the center of her world is the moment he starts to feel less romantic about you.

This is because as soon as the man senses that you've devoted yourself to him exclusively before he's given you the commitment you want, he starts to think less of you.

It's a demonstration of weakness and lack of self-respect to him.

Parting Word of wisdom, and take away for this rule:

Being exclusive with a man does not automatically lead to lasting love and commitment. Keeping your options open and focusing on what you need will.

Rule # 7 Focus on yourself

By focusing on yourself and doing the things that make you feel warm and romantic and wonderful inside, you can completely change your vibe.

Instead of feeling desperate, you feel free. Instead of feeling needy, you feel generous. Dating for the fun of dating, or flirting with other men makes you feel strong inside. It

makes you feel wanted and desirable. Most importantly, it makes you feel that you have choices in how to feel fulfilled and happy.

Rule # 8 Date Yourself: Ellen's story

Early on in Ellen's relationship, when things weren't going well between she and her boyfriend, Ellen tried everything she could think of to fix it. She would talk, plead, and argue with her husband, Jim.

She would think about their problems and what he wanted almost non-stop. Ellen made him the center of her world because as Ellen explained, "I felt so desperate to make it work, but all it did was to push him away even further."

Then a light went off in Ellen's head. She was focusing on the WRONG person! When she stepped back and stopped trying and doing, and just relaxed into her own skin, things completely turned around. Ellen dated herself by doing things that honored what she needed, and can you guess what happened? Her husband, Jim, showed renewed interest, and his feelings changed for her overnight.

Changing the way a man feels around you is as easy as following the Commitment Blue print and the Strategic Dating Rules!

Your transformative experience will occur "like a light going on in your head (like it was in Ellen's), and you'll have you "Ah Ha" moment, too!

You will see immediate results when you practice all the rules and follow the Commitment blueprint that leads you (and your "Mr. Right") to the wedding alter!

As you begin to understand why all of the things you've been taught about dating and relationships (before reading this book) is actually **hurting** your chances for real and lasting love, you'll know exactly what to do instead to bring him with you to the start-line of the path that leads to the wedding alter in 6 months to 1 year!

Fact: No person is going to treat you with more respect than YOU are willing to treat and show yourself. No person is willing to marry you (and put a ring on it) unless you hold yourself to that higher standard, and stick to it. And if they can't (or won't rise to your higher standard) then you must not lower yourself to theirs! Save ...... giving your ALL to the one and only person that is willing to give you their all, legally.

Therefore, If you are in a relationship with a person (and you want to get married) it would be to your advantage to decide your expiration date for being a "girlfriend" and refrain from becoming anybody's "wifee."

Believe it or not, after the first 90 days, both persons in the relationship have decided what their intentions are for moving forward (one way or the other). But you have to be honest and speak up and state your desires, unless of course you are afraid of the answer, and are willing to do whatever it takes to be with that person, and that's your choice. It is never too late for you to hit the re-set button, and start fresh. Just cut your losses. I'm just saying.

Reminder:

Some people come into our lives for a season, and others for a reason. If they want to leave, let them go (with a smile). If you are in an unhappy, lonely relationship ----- you don't have to remain in it. You know that this situation just isn't working out (on so many levels). But you stay because .... blah, blah, blah, blah, blah! Get over it. Have faith, and be of cheer! Let go and Let God! Something good is waiting to happen for you. Cut your losses! Smile! Keep it moving!....and watch your "happy place" come back! If you keep running back to the person you need to walk away from, you'll never create space for the better things to arrive.

CHAPTER 19

FIRST DATE PERCEPTIONS

If you know what to look out for, you could know as early as the first date whether or not a man has potential to be your Mr. Right.

It requires a shift of focus on your part, away from being so preoccupied with impressing him and getting him to like you, onto how he behaves and what he says.

The goal here is to quickly get to know his values so you can make a good decision on whether he's right for you before you waste any time or emotion.

Even though it's a first date, your date is giving off all kinds of clues about his values in his body language, in the way he treats the staff in the restaurant, by how he reacts to unexpected situations, and more?

It's true. No matter how much we want to believe that a guy's bad behavior or undesirable qualities come "out of the blue," they're usually there all along and we don't want (or allow ourselves) to see them.

On the positive side, there are also immediate telltale signs that a man would make an amazing long-term partner – that he will be caring, loving, a good protector and provider…

So that you can confidently know that it's worth investing in this guy.

Are You Coachable?

Which of these are true and to what extent?

1. I usually allow my manager and others to complete their sentences before responding. (If you don't, it's not a good sign.)

2. When I'm given feedback/ criticism, I usually think about it before responding, waiting just a bit. (If you don't, you're likely not giving it real consideration.)

3. When I'm given feedback/ criticism, I rarely find myself defending a position or action immediately. (If this is true, you're probably trying to really learn how you can improve.)

4. When I'm given feedback/ criticism, I ask questions about it in order to try to better understand it. (A good sign.)

5. I feel my work's purpose is to serve my external customers. ("You're gonna have to serve somebody." – Bob Dylan)

6. I feel my work's purpose is to serve my internal customers (managers, colleagues, other departments).

7. I've changed/ revised my position/ approach because of the advice of another individual. (If not, how coachable do you really think you are? No one is always right.)

8. My manager invests time in my professional development (If s/he doesn't, it might be because of a perception that you're un-

coachable).

There's no rating scale here. These questions are simply meant to raise awareness (when answered as objectively and truthfully).

CHAPTER 20

IS HE OUT JUST FOR SEX?

How to tell if he just wants sex?

Almost all guys want sex. So, how do you tell when a guy is only out or sex? How do you spot the ones who don't plan on sticking around ?

Well, the first thing to notice is how he reacts to you denying him sex.

If someone proves to be unworthy of your investment of time, energy or efforts, waste no further time with him and feel glad to have found out sooner rather than later.

The woman who demonstrates her value early on in the relationship is the one who gets pursued beyond sex.

If his reaction is too emotional or angry or upset or he is too persistent about having to have sex right this minute, ditch him!

Basically say to him, "I'm a lady and I don't have sex with men I just met." Simple as that! If he can't respect that, then politely tell him you're not the kind of girl he's looking for. If he starts showing signs of aggravation or anger, then flip it around! Don't lose control! You have to be the one to get upset! You have to be the one that gets aggravated and says, "I have to go" or "that's messed up."

Don't allow the man to be the one who's "disappointed" because he's not getting his way.

YOU are the one that is "disappointed" in HIM for pressuring YOU. If he doesn't stick around after that, then don't sweat it. He was just trying to screw you and he had no real interest in you. He was trying to use you for sex.

You should be proud of yourself for not giving in. You just avoided getting used. Strong, wise women do not get used. If he really likes you, he'll tell you he respects your wishes and he'll stick around.

TRUST ME, when a guy likes you, he will wait for it. Until you've found a man worthy of your affection, a good night kiss is all anyone is getting from you! You must commit to this. Giving up your precious VJJ, oral sex, a hand job, or anything sexually stimulating to a man easily, without making him earn it is the biggest mistake you can make as a woman! You're just giving away your most precious asset for free!

Men of the "ghosting" or the **"disappearing"** kind tend to react emotionally "unreasonable" to being denied sex, and will even break up with the woman **only** if he plans on never having another date with her, developing a relationship that leads to marriage, and/or if he has his own emotional hang-ups that includes "proving" something.

Either way you don't need any part of it. A good rule of thumb is to never punish a guy for wanting sex, but the bigger concern is: if he reacts badly to your denial.

Denying a man sex doesn't have to be done in a mean, formal, way.

You can say no without making him feel rejected.

Just say to him that you really choose not to move that fast, while charmingly throwing approval his way.

The guy who enjoys your company and wants to get to

know you better will have no problem **NOT** having sex on the first second, third, fourth, or a distant future date.

If he is truly interested in pursuing a relationship with you, he will wait until you are ready, without you have to give him any reason.

Mostly, he'll just need some type of intimate progression as the two of you grow closer, and develop a strong foundation for your relationship, and future together.

If he's reached an emotionally point, and you have become a woman like no other in his eyes, the actual sex can wait.

A sign of his emotional security, as he demonstrates his confidence that it (sex with you) will happen eventually.

Weather it happens tomorrow, next week, or next month, or several months, he knows it will happen.

Your denial (of sex with him) will not concern him if he feels a connection to you, especially one of value to him.

Time with you becomes worth waiting for a physical relationship with him

This is a good reason for denying a guy sex on a first date if nothing else. It allows you to see whether he plans on having another (date with you or not).

When you have a requirement of 60 – 90 days, for example, you will definitely weed out the players that are out to score, with beautiful, smart women like us.

Don't play hard to get!

Be hard to get! You must establish boundaries for having sex with your special guy that you plan to marry! He'll value you forever! A sophisticated woman assumes that all healthy guys will desire her sexually, but she doesn't allow her understanding of his basic urge to want to sleep with her dictate how she behaves.
What she does is engages with him, and all men in general, on her own terms!

Here's an example: Suppose your suitor (or boyfriend) calls you up at 10:00 p.m. and ask you to come over to his place?

A smart woman will know that that is a booty call and is never the way to gain respect, or help establish a genuine relationship. Always turn don't an invitation of this nature.

Your guy doesn't mind if sex isn't in the cards right away, when you're adding value to his life.

Be your charming self, and be inspired to know that as long as he still feels like he's in the game, and he's got something to look forward too, it doesn't matter.

You have become that unforgettable woman that he is worried about keeping. He is not concerned about being made to wait (to have sex with you). How to prove himself to you in ways that will get you to say yes to a marriage proposal, will soon be on his mind, instead.

If he's focused on sex, you need to be focused on expressing your value and representing your "brand" well.

From a casual date with, cooking a meal together, walking down to a local coffee shop, or even just hanging out together reading the Sunday paper or catching up on some work on your laptops, opportunities overflow for both displaying your value and connecting emotionally (with him).

When a guy continues to press you to come over at night, you know immediately that he isn't interested in investing more in the relationship.

If he continues to pressure you for sex say this:

Tell him you're offended because he's trying to GUILT you into sex and you don't like men that do that. Tell him he's making you feel uncomfortable. Do and say whatever is necessary to flip the guilt back to him. You must do this to retain the control. You should also do this because now that he's had a tiny sample, he's going to go crazy over you!

If you only give a man a little piece of action, he's going to fantasize about it over and over again. You're going to be the most desirable thing to him. He won't be able to think straight. Mesmerize that man with your pussy powers.

What to say if he tries to talk you into having oral sex with him:

When first dating a man, you shouldn't be having any kind of sex with him, especially oral sex. If a guy is expecting oral sex, you can just tell him straight out: "I don't go down on guys. I would only do that with someone I'm in a deeply committed relationship with." And you and I are not there, yet!

If a man has a problem with that, don't worry one second about it! **He was just trying to use you for a blow job!**

An Important Rule You Must Follow: Protect your health! Do not, under any circumstance, have oral sex with random men.

The second you go down on a man, you have just lost his respect. **Save** oral sex for the special man that earns and deserves it: **your husband, only!**

Oral sex should be even harder to get than regular (vaginal) sex! When you find a good man and he's everything you ever wanted, save the oral sex for him.

If this is your "Mr. Right, he'll respect you and your rationale. **This will bring you to the wedding alter much quicker too!**

Again, if he has problem with it, you've got your answer.

He was just trying to use you for a blow job!

You win: Before he disappeared!

CHAPTER 21

SIGNS THAT A MAN IS READY AND INTERESTED IN DEVELOPING A RELATIONSIP WITH YOU

There are 4 signs you should look for that will indicate his readiness for a relationship

1. Trying to integrate you with his friends and family

If he makes an effort to get you involved with his social circle, you know he's thinking further ahead than a few dates.

Once a guy is ready to be with you seriously, he'll want his friends and family to be aware of it; getting you involved with them is his way of saying that he has chosen you as something more than just a fling.

If on the other hand he is keen to keep you away at all costs, it might spell out that he doesn't want you getting the wrong idea.

2. Planning a trip with just the two of you

Any sign of a vacation or going for a "weekend away" somewhere is a sure sign that a guy wants something more.

It's not just about the money; it symbolizes and emotional investment on his part, since he's spent time planning and thinking about something you can both do together. Guys don't do this kind of thing for girls they're not serious about.

3. Going out of his way to plan a special date

The more he goes out of the way to plan special dates, the more you know he wants to impress you with his creativity (which is of course, a good sign).

But if, on the other hand, he only plans dates which never require him to go out of his way (i.e. he only asks you to come over to his place, or to the pub 5 minutes away from his house) then it's likely this guy only wants you when it's convenient for him.

4. Talking about future plans

Notice if he always avoids talking about plans more than a week in advance, or if he shifts nervously when you mention something the two of you might do in the future. If he's happy to say little things like "We should have dinner there next time" or "We'll have more time when work is less busy next month," this is the kind of talk that makes you know he feels comfortable with seeing you two together for a while, so look out for the signals.

So there you have it: The one indicator (and four signs) you can use to tell if he's ready to move forward to commit to a relationship.

CHAPTER 22

KEEP HIS INTEREST PEAKED

Keeping a guy interested long-term and understanding what they want can be tricky at times.

You'll probably notice guys avoiding certain questions when it comes to taking things to the next step when dating, so tread carefully and use your good judgement. In order to keep a guy and stay on his mind, and never disappears (like some men may have done in the past). There are some things that NEVER work! Don't do either one of these things.

None of these work! Don't waste your time:

A. Trying harder never works. In fact it makes you look too needy.
B. Going "cold" get less emotional close your heart off
C. Wait and hope. You Stay on his terms. You become the giver and he the taker
D. Try to make him jealous. You are seen as unstable not to be trusted
E. Giving him an ultimatum to force him to do it.

CHAPTER 23

WHEN DATING RULES ARE BROKEN

This interview actually occurred, however, the name of the participant has been changed to protect their identity.Weeping, Willow, contacted me at 2:30 a.m. in the morning.

Rita J. Jackson: Hello Willow. Please provide more Information, and background on the topic.

Willow: Well I basically am a bit hurt and crushed about a connection that has come to an abrupt ending and It was not a long standing one

Willow: I am 35 and the man Is 34, we are both working professionals. In *****I am from ***** and he is from ****.

I met him In July and I have not felt a strong connection like this In 7 years. He seemed to be interested but warned me that 2 years ago his relationship ended, and he was not sure he was ready for a serious relationship which I was not asking for but he seemed to feel I expected right away. I assume because of the way we connected.

Willow: It is a very common, natural and human situation I am dealing with-and I must accept and let go. It ended by this weekend- we have not seen one another since June as he went to ------- for business and I have had holidays (I am a teacher) and was traveling with family. I am not married-I mean my mom and brother-and we had been in touch and

Rita J. Jackson: I see. So what is it that you wish to have assistance with?

Willow: I don't know his reasons for pulling back and I am not sure how to process it, other than assume he Is afraid to get Involved again and get hurt.

Rita J. Jackson: Tell me how long you were together, and while together were you Intimate with him?

Willow: Not long at all. Yes. I was. We met by chance one evening while I was stood up on a date and went out with a girlfriend of mine to forget about things-he was out celebrating his birthday with friends. We ended up meeting and going back to his place. The next day I stayed all morning and the day after that I went to his place for dinner that he made and we talked all night and then made love.

Willow: I know how this sounds-not long, very quick, etc.

Willow: But I am honest when I say with all my experience I have never felt swept off my feet before.

Willow: And that Is what we agreed to and then he backed away saying he felt I was chasing something he could not provide.

Rita J. Jackson: You said that he told you that he felt that he could not provide what you were in need of (from his point of view). Trust and believe him what he has told you. It might be very hard to accept what he has said, but you would be smart to cut your loss, now. The best thing for you to do at this point is to stay calm for a while and do not chase after him. In due time he may come back and be with you. It will require time for you to actually be sure that he felt something more than passion, In the moment.

Willow: He told me he found me smart, beautiful, and had a lot to give.

Willow: He told me sex was not the motivation for inviting me for an evening with him and that is why he divulged so much about his life with me. So yes, I know what you are saying. Also.

Willow: Bear in mind I am not clueless either. I am well educated, well-traveled and have a life of my own.

Rita J. Jackson: Nevertheless, and ever the more, there are dating rules, and there is one very important one that it appears (from what you've told me) you skipped over one very important one: the courtship (and the chase) Men tend to value and hold on to what they have worked to earn.

Willow: You think he just felt chased by my behavior and lost Interest In me?

Willow: Well I met him while we were both under the Influence of alcohol.

Willow: Yes

Willow: Well he seemed pretty clear that he did not want to have a relationship with me and asked me not to contact him. He was angry. So In other words I blew It and he felt I was desperate, even though he said the contrary to me Is what you are saying?

Rita J. Jackson: It appears that he may be pulling back for fear of getting In quicker than he wanted to do so.

Willow: Well should I text to say: I get It, you didn't have to work for me and therefore you don't value me. I get It, hunter mentality. I blew It. see ya.

Rita J. Jackson: You should quit texting him.

Rita J. Jackson: I hope that you won't take It personal. Just know that It will take so time to have the relationship that you deserve. You actually acted on your emotions, as did he. Unfortunately, in this case, several relationship building rules were broken, so quickly that it has negatively affected the outcome of "getting your guy!" Right now, the best thing that you can do, is be

patient. "Chill out!"

Willow: Do you honestly think there Is any chance he will come back? I apologized to him after he got angry. I actively work on keeping anxiety and depression at bay. I am confident and a beautiful, smart woman but I do have trouble being vulnerable when I sense I followed my Instinct and It lead me Into a position where I am waiting for a man to approach me. I feel stupid and dumb. like It Is my fault. I am easy, not cheap.

Willow: He Is not going to contact me again. I was too easy.

Willow: He Is not going to contact me again.

Willow: He thinks I am desperate and not worth It.

Rita J. Jackson: He may or may not. However, what is important is how you

react (with him and guys that you meet) form this point in time. You have the ability to get it right from this point on. In our next session we can discuss where do you go from here, and positives ways to use what you learned from this experience.

Willow: It is not that he is scared about getting hurt. I was not mysterious and challenging enough, because I was authentic and open.

Willow: If he does contact me...then....what do you advice?

Rita J. Jackson: Do NOT act in ways that show you to be desperate, clingy, or try to use him as your analyst. Telling him all about you past hurtful experiences (including the one that you just had with him) is definitely NOT cool! A man can see the difference.

Willow: He said I was crazy. That I knew him for 2 days and spoke to him like he had been with me for years. So there is no way I did not blow It. Well he didn't call me crazy but said it.

Rita J. Jackson: When he sees that you are NOT crazy, and that you can keep yourself together, and function with or without him.

Willow: So how long are you suggesting? A month?

Rita J. Jackson: I can't predict the future. It could be soon or several months (or never). The best thing that you can do is to be good to yourself, and move forward with your life. Don't wait around for him to come back! When or if he does come back, it should be to a newly empowered version of you! A woman that is in control of her emotions!

Willow: He will not hear anything about me...so I feel I blew this one...really badly...

Rita J. Jackson: Just stop contacting and texting him. Fill your time with fun and interesting activities.

Willow: I did...I really blew it...and I am sad because I really like him and I feel like I just fucked It all up. I am so embarrassed and he knows this.

Rita J. Jackson: I can feel your pain, and I am aware of your emotional investment, too. In the meantime, don't continue to beat yourself up!

Willow: ok

Self-assessment

- Summarize and list the relationship rules that Willow broke.

CHAPTER 24

PRESSURE TO HAVE SEX

If it has only been a couple or three weeks (or even worse, just one date) and a man starts pressuring you to have sex, **you can deal with his pressure** with one easy statement:

Basically say to him, "I'm a lady and I don't have sex with men I just met." Simple as that! If he can't respect that, then politely tell him you're not the kind of girl he's looking for. If he starts showing signs of aggravation or anger, then flip it around! Don't lose control! You have to be the one to get upset! You have to be the one that gets aggravated and says, "I have to go" or "that's messed up." Don't allow the man to be the one who's "disappointed" because he's not getting his way. YOU are the one that is "disappointed" in HIM for pressuring YOU. If he doesn't stick around after that, then don't sweat it. He was just trying to screw you and he had no real interest in you. He was trying to use you for sex. You should be proud of yourself for not giving in. You just avoided getting used. Strong, wise women do not get used. If he really likes you, he'll tell you he respects your wishes and he'll stick around. TRUST ME, when a guy likes you, he will wait for it. Make up in your mind that: **Until you've found a man worthy of your affection, a good night kiss is all anyone is getting from you! And if he ghost or disappears on you, so what? It' may happen, but you won't be emotionally invested!**

CHAPTER 25

IS HE SERIOUS ABOUT YOU

Things that let you know that he is a "timewaster" and never be serious about you.

1. Taking too long to be in an "official" relationship. The commitment just isn't there. He has never made his intentions with you know to you or anybody else.

2. Maintaining separate lives. They don't have any bills or children or bank accounts together. Nothing connected together. You don't know their family well (or at all). Makes it easy for you to go your separate lives. If you don't do things for their mom and they do things for yours. They are not serious about you. You decide to leave, there is no connection.

3. No idea what they want out of a relationship. When a man doesn't have a standard or plan of how a relationship should work best for you and him together, or in general, this is a real indicator that he is not interested in being in one. When asked what he feels a woman role is in a relationship, and he doesn't have a clue, then he usually doesn't have a clue of what your purpose or value is to him in a relationship. They don't know what your purpose is (to him) either, in the long haul, because he

is not planning on that with or for you. If you ask him about family roles, head of the house roles, where would he like to live, and how an ideal relationship ought to work, for example would he prefer a 50/50 relationship or does he see himself being the breadwinner, and you staying home with the kids And he has no thoughts or opinion about any of this, then you know that he can't be serious about you because he doesn't have a plan for you or developing a real meaningful relationship.

Red Flag!

Protect your heart, and do not get too emotionally invested in him. If this sounds like your guy, sooner or later, he may disappear, ghost out, or cheat on you.

CHAPTER 26

THINGS THAT WILL MAKE HIM WANT TO STAY WITH YOU

Men and women have a different thought pattern.

Men think, if I marry you will you become a much larger version of who you are now? Stop having sex? Get comfortable? No guy has been planning their wedding for the past year, like women do in many cases.
For him to get married to you, you'll have to make it worth his while.

Face it, some men stay with women because they need to be in a female lead relationship. They are shy, and they would rather not make the decisions. This type of man enjoys letting the woman "call the shots, all of them!
However, if you are attracted to strong, alpha – personality type males, keep reading:

You have to go through a series of steps.

1. Put yourself into a position that they feel that they cannot do without you.
2. Be on focus with their dream, and believe in their dream.

3. Gain allies. Have a good relationship with members of his family and friends. He will listen to his inner circle. These are people that he respects.
4. Don't be vindictive. Don't try to hurt him. Just be cool. Be nice. Upgrade yourself. Take care of yourself. Keep putting forth an effort to put a smile on the face of your guy.
5. Make yourself indispensable. So that he believes that he would never find anybody better than you.

CHAPTER 27

FANTASY VERSUS REALITY

Sometimes, it's not until you let go of the "Mr. Right" in your fantasy (the one you dream about in your mind) that you'll be able to actually get HAPPY in the reality of the here and now.

Furthermore, and sometimes, it is the pursuit of your original passion (or fantasy "Mr. Right") that has actually made you a bit jaded, rough around the edges, or MISERABLE.

Admittedly so, you may attract your fantasy "Mr. Right" guy, but if it only happens for 1% of most men and women, it is wise to figure out a workable Plan B.

Her romantic fantasy might be something along these lines?

Is he 6'1", blue eyes, wavy brown hair, broad shoulders, fit abs?

Does he play guitar, paint, surf, write, appreciate art, and know how to salsa?

Is he well-read, highly educated, confident, charismatic, intuitive and generous?

Does he knock your socks off in bed? Is he a super father? A strong communicator?

Is his passport well used? Can he lead and take control? Does he make you laugh?

Will he make over $500,000 so he can get out of work whenever he wants and you have the option of whether you ever want to work again?

We can go on, but we don't have to. You have an idea of the kind of man you want.

You've been holding out for him your whole life.

He is her dreams, her passion, and her fantasy.

And he's making her miserable.

On the rare occasion she meets this man, and it either turns out that:

1. He's not interested in you.

2. He's interested in sleeping with you, but not in dating you.

3. He's interested in dating you, but doesn't treat you well.

4. He treats you well, but he doesn't want to commit.

Whether it's 1, 2, 3, or 4, you know that what I'm saying is true.

She's holding out for a dream man who does not want to marry her.

And until she lets go of that concept of her dream "Mr. Right" man and start appreciating the men who DO want her, she will continue to make herself unhappy.

I call this "Expectation Depression."

The assumption that you have a certain type of man and you couldn't be happy with any man who deviates from that type.

You expect the sun, the moon and the stars from men and then become despondent that life doesn't conform to your unrealistic expectations.

Finally, the second a woman let's go of the fantasy, "Mr. Right" dream guy, is the second she realizes that her new reality is BETTER than the old one and she finds true love.

CHAPTER 28

FIRST IMPRESSION TIPS

So here are five things you must know immediately if you want to win a guy over when you meet up with him:

1. Men are drawn to women with a joy for life

Do you greet him warmly? Do you smile and show you're excited about the date? Do you seem like someone who has a passionate life?

A guy is noticing all these things when you introduce yourself.

If you give him a limp-wristed handshake and have a neutral uninterested look, he'll assume you're going to be a major downer rather than someone who brings positivity and general good vibes into his world.

I just used the term "good vibes" and I kind of hate myself for it. But it's true.

Guys are praying you'll be easy to talk to. They are crossing their fingers hoping you'll have a big smile and a great energy.

That guy you've just met is hoping you'll answer his questions enthusiastically and show you're the kind of person who is excited about what he's doing.

It sounds like a lot of pressure, but really, this is what everyone should be like who lives with passion.

2. He wants to see you're interested

One thing guys notice very quickly is whether a woman is self-involved or interested in getting to know him better.

If you don't ask any questions or seem like you want to hear more about who he is, it makes him feel distant and he'll quickly be turned off.

It's easy to fall into a passive mode of answering questions without reciprocating and showing genuine interest in the other person. Watch out for this trap in any interaction.

Yes, men are often doing the impressing on a date, but he needs to see that you are intrigued by him as well.

3. Men want a woman who is self-expressive

How closed is your body language? Do you tend to hold back from expressing yourself or laughing or giving an opinion?

When a guy feels like you're holding back, he feels like he's not getting to the more vulnerable part of your personality that reveals your authentic self.

If you have defensive barriers or you get uncomfortable with real conversation, he'll often interpret this as insecurity, which is a huge turn-off on a first date.

If you want to date a confident guy, it's crucial to show you are comfortable with being expressive and showing your authentic self.

4. Guys care about your attention to detail

Women are turned off by sloppy, disheveled appearance and so are men.

When he first sees you for a date there's a good chance that he's wondering "Did she make an effort to look attractive?"

You don't have to always show up in the tiny red dress you save for formal dinners, but if you're rocking up in ill-fitted jeans and a hoodie, no matter how pretty he finds you, he's going to be asking himself whether you're someone he could be attracted to long-term.

While it may be true that guys are more often the culprits for being bad dressers, but remember that you never get a second chance to make a first impression! ……..And men do notice! I know! It's the quality and confidence of a person that makes you stand up and take notice of someone as something other than a friend.

It's the slight glint in your eye or the warm hug when you meet them that makes you aware of their body for half a second.

It's being comfortable with contact, even if it's a tiny touch on the hand or arm.

It may be more accurate here to say physical confidence, but either way, it's this that really changes you from a potential friend in a guy's head to someone he thinks about sexually.

Now that you know how to make a guy want you in the first minute, you can nail that important first impression armed with the knowledge of exactly how to push his romantic buttons.

If you tend to be highly successful, independent, and over-functioning, there is a good chance that you are an **Alpha Female**.

Alpha -personality type women can often be intimidating to those around her and isn't afraid to ask for what she wants. She's killing it in her career and has a solid group of friends to rely on.

There's nothing quite as brilliant as a woman with confidence and ambition. She isn't scared to put people in their place should they do her dirty, nor is she willing to put up with anyone else's donkey -doo! She simply doesn't have the time.

A strong Alpha Woman needs a man who's her equal, her partner, her greatest supporter. By definition, you'd think that she should want an Alpha Male, but he can provide only passion, not steadiness. She also doesn't get along with Beta Males because they're too weak to keep her or pique her interest.

So, who's right for the mighty Alpha Female? What kind of man can keep her grounded while still challenging her to grow and be the best she can?

Drum roll please: Introducing Type Z: a man who's equal parts solid and charismatic. He's her rock, her foundation. He's not intimidated by her successes nor would he allow her to walk all over him. He's true to himself and true to her. An Alpha Woman knows what she needs to have a sturdy partnership with a man who'll be her ally, her confidant and her best friend.

CHAPTER 29

BOYFRIEND TRAITS THAT MATCH ALPHA FEMALES:

1. He'd never be malicious or say something to hurt your feelings, but he can give a joke just as well as you can.

He's someone who can tease you and also be teased.
You know each other well enough to know when you've crossed the line, but your shared love of sarcasm and your knowledge of each other's weak spots make teasing fun — never threatening.

2. Life with him is always exciting and never ceases to surprise you. He challenges you.

He's as strong as you are, but more subdued. He'll push you to be the best you can be and challenge every decision you make — but you'll love him for it.

3. He doesn't get jealous.

He's confident enough to know that the mild flirtations you have at a cocktail party and your unyielding friendship with your work husband are never a threat to your relationship.

He knows you're his and never feels the need to question you because your relationship was built on a foundation of trust.

4. He's a source of comfort for you.

He isn't waiting on you, he has his own plans.

He has his own life and respects that you have yours. He's never going to give you a hard time about wanting to hit the club with your girls.

Instead, he encourages you to spend time with them whenever you want to because he knows whom you're coming home to.

5. He doesn't air your dirty laundry.

He has your full trust, and you can tell each other anything. You're not afraid your embarrassing stories are going to come back to you when you meet his family or when you meet his friends for drinks.

What's said between the two of you stays between the two of you. Well, except for your BFF; she knows everything from what he's got going on downstairs to his latest promotion at work.

6. He knows how to deal with your bad moods.

You feel at ease with him. When you're angry, he somehow knows how to deal with you with more grace than anyone else.

Depending on how you're feeling, impatient, and emotional or overwhelmed and exhausted, he lets you have your space and knows when to hold you in his arms.

7. When he apologizes, he really means it.

If he's done something wrong, he'll always be man enough to admit it and tell you he's sorry. He's not arrogant or pigheaded — he won't do something unacceptable and turn the tables on you, and he won't hurt your feelings and make you feel stupid for being upset.

He's a man, not a boy — and a man always knows when he needs to apologize.

8. He's moving at the same speed you are.

Whether in his current career or his lofty life goals, he always seems to be moving at the same speed you are. He knows what he wants and respects what you want. He's never pushy or demoralizing — just steadily moving from one goal to the next with a very bright future in sight.

9. He doesn't belittle you, but he doesn't put you on pedestal either.

He's slow and steady, but never a doormat. He doesn't idolize you but doesn't make you feel small. He treats you like the fierce woman you are. He also likes to spoil you, but would never give you everything you want.

He'll always keep you guessing. He's your partner, not your provider. He's there because he wants you, not because he needs you.

10. You learn from him in many ways, but you never feel like he's pushing you or judging you.

He is someone who teaches, but never lectures.

The best partnerships are the ones in which both people can learn from each other. He's a well of knowledge and loves to provide you with new information and insights on things he's passionate about.

You both teach other lessons that make you better people and better citizens of the world.

11. Your shared love of sarcasm and his sharp wit complement each other perfectly.

He makes you laugh.

If he doesn't make you laugh, you'll soon grow tired of him. Laughter is one of the most important qualities in a partner.

12. He'll never fail to tell you how it is.

He'll call you out when you need to be called out.

He's not scared to hurt your feelings, and he doesn't tiptoe around you, either. If you're acting like a raging b*tch or are completely talking out of your ass, you can bet your ass he'll call you out on it.

He doesn't let you get away with silliness/donkey-doo, not because he's a tough guy, but because he doesn't want to be jerked around by those Alpha Female ways.

13. He wants to be the wind beneath your wings.

He's a stoic man: strong, independent and sure of himself. He prefers to let you lead, but he's always there to fully support you. He has no problem being the background; he's there to be your strongest supporter and your steadfast foundation. He loves that you're popular because you're a person he's very proud of.

14. He lets you be the social butterfly you naturally are .

He isn't the life of the party, but is always there if you need to be carried home.

. He doesn't mind your vibrancy or doesn't feel intimidated by your fiery, dynamic personality; instead, he embraces it. He's also a protector.

He'll pour you another drink, but take it away when you've had too much. He always takes care of you.

15. His opinions aren't irrational, they're backed up.

He reads a whole lot of books and stays informed on current events so he can have well-rounded opinions with factual bases. Being educated and sound in his understanding of the world around him is very important to him.

16. He knows when to drop it and when to address it.

He'll stand his ground when he knows he is right. Though he'll argue with you, he's not unwilling to concede if it means ending a fight. You're strong-willed, and he knows when a difference in opinion or a questionable action is worth discussing or whether it's better left alone.

17. He has dreams as big as yours.

He's as career-focused as you are. You both genuinely care about each other's endeavors. He doesn't sit back and watch you achieve your dreams because he has passions and goals of his own. You two are a true power couple.

18. He's a great listener, but also expects to be heard.

He knows when to talk and he knows when to keep his mouth shut. He quietly and patiently listens to everything you have to say, but he expects you to do the same for him.

FINAL NOTE

Once you're able to let go of previous ways of thinking about men and dating, a completely new world awaits you. You'll never waste your time again with ineligible suitors, including and not limited to men that won't commit for any number of reasons.

You'll have men lining up to date you, desperate for your attention, and eager to please you! You'll never be sad over men again! You won't be cheated on lied to, or let down by men ever again.

Your "Mr. Right" will find you! In fact, he may be someone that you already have a friendship with! Check out the men that already like you, and are always there for you! Trust me, you can easily make him fall madly in love with you, and never want to leave you. Best of all you'll be having the time of your life while doing it! ~ Rita Richardson Jackson

Booking information:

To contact Rita Richardson for **Book signings, public appearances, workshops**

Email: dateandlaugh@gmail.com

ATIR Publishing: Book orders (in bulk)

Email atirglobal@gmail.com

On sale through:

Amazon: http://www.amazon.com/Marriage-Demand-Singles-Interested-Getting/dp/0692543651/ref=sr_1_1?s=books&ie=UTF8&qid=1460003506&sr=1-1&keywords=rita+richardson+jackson

ATIR Publishing: Email atirglobal@gmail.com

Online: www.livepersonexperts.com and Email atirglobal@gmail.com to order in bulk

ABOUT THE AUTHOR

Rita Richardson Jackson ~ Life Coach / Therapist Online / Author / Motivational Speaker

Change agent, motivator, and leader are the words that have been used to describe Rita Richardson Jackson. Ms. Rita J. gained international notoriety in 2014, after she expanded her clientele via the internet.

Rita J. points to her own life as proof that mentoring is the answer and that success is a choice. Growing up in an upper middle class family in Bessemer, Alabama, Rita J. witnessed firsthand the important effects of having a professional role model to offer the guidance that every young woman needs and vowed to help provide that to others.

Rita J. completed college and received a Bachelors of Arts Degree in Biology from Miles College in Birmingham / Fairfield, Alabama. She then went on to attend the Ohio State University Columbus and received a Master of Arts degree in Health Education with a focus in Human Sexuality. Since then, she has completed additional post graduate certifications at Fowler International Academy, Harvard University JFK School of Business, Miami University, and the Ohio State University.

In addition, she holds certificates as Certified Life Coach, from Fisher International Academy and trained with the internationally known Sex Experts Masters & Johnson, St Louis, MO., and completed Sexual Attitude Reassessment training at the Kinsey Institute, in Bloomington, IL.

The inspiration Ms. Rita J. provides to her clients and professional associates is effective in motivating each and every individual to believe in themselves, connect to their purpose and have faith in their ability to navigate transition. Rita is a gifted motivational speaker, Life Coach, and Therapist who holds audiences, and her clients spellbound while sharing with them solid strategies to help <u>them reach their professional and personal goals. Rita J. Jackson</u> is a leader, and top rated life Coach and Therapist delivering compelling, life-changing motivational keynotes and seminar presentations to businesses and corporations, too. Her engaging and entertaining messages challenge and inspire her audience, and clients, too.

More than a keynote speaker, Life Coach, and Therapist, Rita J. is an organizational strategist that inspires greatness in the workplace. From front-line employees to executive leadership teams, Rita J's strategies have proven to be successful in helping employees grow from "Good to Great," and her clients are always led to in solution focused sessions.

Book Ms. Rita J. to INSPIRE your Group, facilitate a Marriage Work Works Workshop, a Speed Dating Event, or a Girls' Night Out Sip & See Social: Email: atirglobal@gmail.com or simply inbox: Rita Richardson Jackson, on Facebook.

Made in the USA
Charleston, SC
09 May 2016